Apocalyptic, awe-filled, riveting. The poems of Eva Hooker's *Godwit* will leave you breathless, confounded by their lush pastoral gorgeousness juxtaposed against a grief-stricken, kaleidoscopic examination of the soul whose "haunt is wilderness." An exciting, erratic, electrically-charged pulse runs through these poems and their startling exploration of nature, beauty, desire, and of language itself, where "Meaning is such hard country." Hooker boldly confronts the very essence of knowledge, of life and death, in rapturous sequences that resist closure in the name of inquiry, innovation, and formal daring. The lyric ruptures, fractures in shimmering pools of grief. Never has the natural world—columbine, lady slipper, trillium, bloodroot—been so devastatingly and excruciatingly alive.

—HADARA BAR-NADAV, *Lullaby (with Exit Sign)*

I am a delighted reader of Eva Hooker's wonderful book, *Godwit*. Body, spirit; sacred, profane; art, life—they are all here in abundance, but as continuities, not dualities. Hooker's delicacy of touch, her prosody, the entire poetics of her project, will win the attention of anyone with an ear for the music of words.

—JOHN MATTHIAS, *Trigons*

In *Godwit*, Eva Hooker's voice is resonant with the presences of Hopkins, Herbert, Dickinson, Levertov, but creates a music entirely her own: a love of this world and glimpses of another.

—MARY GORDON, *The Liar's Wife: Four Novellas*

The extraordinary poems in Eva Hooker's *Godwit* examine and map desire as the impetus for creation and the discovery of form—in nature, in loss, in the soul, in the grammar of the heart. Positioned "on the margins between what is mortal/and what is not," these poems open from mutable worlds we know into those we thought were invisible, ineffable, but what might very well contain the marks of our own humanity. Artful, luminous, and intellectually fierce, this work is transformative.

—MARY PINARD, *Portal*

Godwit marks a meeting place, between the long-legged bird and the prairie marsh, the back-lit city and fields of blue aster, plain speech and numinous revelation. Here sublime beauty, fraught with shadows, calls readers "to pick our way through radiance with dirty shoes." In charged language and a strikingly modern sensibility, Eva Hooker's eloquent poems undertake the ancient task of soul-making.

—PATRICIA KIRKPATRICK, *Odessa*

GODWIT

GODWIT
EVA HOOKER

POEMS

THREE: A TAOS PRESS

First U.S. edition 2016

Design by Castro Watson

Cover Art: *A Black-Tailed Godwit* by Aert Schouman
© Crispian Riley-Smith Fine Arts Ltd.

Author Photograph by Rebecca Stull, Little Wing Creative

Printed in the United States of America by Cottrell Printing Company

ISBN: 978-0-9847925-9-7

THREE: A TAOS PRESS
P.O. Box 370627
Denver, CO 80237
www.3taospress.com

10 9 8 7 6 5 4 3 2 1

For my sister, Tina

OF GOD SALT

DARK IS THE SHADOW OF ME

THERE IS WORK TO DO WITHIN NOTHINGNESS

GODWIT

OF GOD SALT

All these things entered you
As if they were both the door and what came through it.
They marked the spot, marked time and held it open.

—SEAMUS HEANEY

PRAIRIE, UNDER FULL MOON

In the blooming period, everywhere is open.
Winds make you arrive where you do not want to go.

Disrupt the
Sequence of the hours.

Everything starts talking: bract, awn, butterfly,
Godwit.

~

You collide with the place,
Leave tattooed and bone crackled.

Even the chickens shout. Such that these are called
Booming grounds.

The sun appears to set unexpectedly.
The earth, to widen and shrink to a moving flatness,

As if Jacob's ladder were built sideways.
Angels roam restlessly

Anxious to deliver
Their burden. They make crossings of weird

Gravity and synaptic light.

~

You see words are not always accurate.

Sometimes they are prone
To excess. And mutiny. What does the body mean to say

By trembling?

~

O sparrow, speak the bird's O until the breath runs out

You can read your wound. Its hidden seam.
Its slip-knot.

MANTRA

Assist me with signification let me translate into another:
read it as mercy.

~

[And talk (why?) with mute ash]: the tree lies as it falls—

~

Death arrives full shriven
of gravity

Speaking a formal
tongue: separation from the body.

~

[And talk (why?) with mute ash]: the tree lies as it falls—

~

Columbine blooms red in the night.
And thou not there—

Read it as mercy.

ANALOGY OF THE BEE AND THE SOUL
Lady Slipper, Cypripedioideae

As when the bee, making
its trespass, slips through the fissure

into the pouch (*labellum*) of the flower and cannot exit,
and, instead, must pass,

carrying over under the stigma,
leaving behind

the pollen it carries. And as it finds,
finally, the door out,

(*it is our unshieldedness
on which we depend so that we may turn out*

into the Open), it brushes
past the anthers, moving in a zigzag, collecting

its new burden
from that interval of closed-up-ness, as if it has lost the art

of looking, (learned
as someone said, so slowly), and also heaviness,

though pollen be light,
so light; it feels for the threshold of the slipper, its margins

and lexicon (*who has twisted
around us like this?*),

lingering (*with all its eyes the natural world looks out*)
in the brackets:

[Only our eyes are turned backward and surround things like traps.]

So the soul of woman, drumming
(*my prayer is growing ripe*), wintering

through absence of doors—
(the wall was not opened by the Doorkeeper,

who laid bare the difficulty, its
harshness—), (she looked

attentively at these things—), now honeyed,
and distillate,

crawls, wanting back and wanting
forward, a

simultaneity, a work of the eye. Then she breaks
to measured

inflorescence,
the flower of her hushed, and scattering, like the bee,

taking the dark
in and out of herself as if to meet her habitat,

its breath, its green finger within her body, then going
further within—

And to burn and to keep and to configure:
she is rare.

Her haunt is wilderness.

MERCY AS A FORM OF ECONOMY

Things that want to step into a name step forward,
Come before the eyes,
Ask for measure, size and weight—

(You carry your bones all wither and rue
(You carry your bones all wither and rue

I stencil cages by hand rifle pyramids for treasure
As if I could make

Pity something I could want.

In the summer I lay on the deck watching the sky move.
I was weary from errands of the dead.

Mosquitoes buzzed.

:: *Within nothing you can occur within*
Nothing you can
occur ::

I remember the blood-bloom how it wastes into beauty.

How this watch is a form
Of death

A practice you perfect
Even as you break molecule from molecule peeling off reciprocity
Like layers of an onion.

We keep within the damaged spellings

                              A quiet zone.

Set the table
Simply with green apples and lemon.

It is the time of the lamb
And anise.

                        Lay down the ligament of your right hand.
Ask mother about lungs

How to breathe how to spill stop yield.
(Your heart is Pentecostal)

Ask if skin is decipherable or the soul so grooved it can carve
                        A self from the inside out.

You can make use of nothing and write with your tongue.

Careful work, this.
Careful work, this.
Careful work, this.

Like writing in the trees when it rains.
It shelters as it washes.

The wild geese do not know that winter will crush their skeletons.

COLUMBINE, WILD
Aquilegia canadensis

*The strength of our souls awaits your coming
in the tent of meeting.*

—Hildegard of Bingen

Drawn out of home   hovering

She speaks   mouth to mouth

All-hallowed and boned   here, she says, here

In slow motion   her agility

Like the full moon   rising

Beyond the petals & sepals   these bones

Are the whole   house murmuring

~

Grief alters the   composition of the air

Breath and honey-suckle   mere current

Pass back and forth   through yellow

Stamens   lift seed and

Fossil   to nodding scarlet   shatter-blossom

BLAZING STAR, WILD
Liatris spicata

Turning towards a soul, it is difficult
To think well, held to

Your purpose like a woman who can see the invisible,
And rest lightly within the given:

A necessary color,
It wants to ride on your back:

(Both *Aria*, *Sarabande*, and crown
Of thorns)—. Out of which you make

Firasa, the capacity to leap
From the known to the unknown, also even

The art of finding
Your way in the desert—:

I have spread my incarnation over you

        [bone of my bone]

        [flesh of my flesh]

        [one body]

Winter, like a wing of wondrous breadth and length

Full of eyes on all sides

SALT FLOWER

Like a floating
Restlessness, alive
& tender.

So this: in the flat.
Think of it as
Salt—

From stain, thin
And papery,
A splaying

Open into
Stars, she, skimming
The sluices open,

Quick & generous,
Her dress hitched
For give.

What if the will
were husk entirely,
and the husk,
breakable,
were broken open, to
where the seeds are? what
then? what would the seeds
be?

It is as they
Said it was: the plowman
Sings of tether,

So pure, so bare, so
Detached, it is
Not prior to

Anything and
Never no where
Without.

It is only that which
Explodes
In the mouth. You.

TRILLIUM
T. grandiflorum

       Solitary, like a pale star.
White-washed flower. They called you Birth-root.

     Woman's secret:
You enable the womb, remind it: within the female body

There is always preparation for another body.

      [The *is* of metaphor is an apology to silence.]

        ~

"Someone has to be there," writes Kafka, "someone has to keep watch."

        ~

     Ants carry your seed to the underground.

And so, *nox*—:

You shall love the nothing you shall
Flee the something you shall stand alone and shall go to no one.

Hunger is what you need to move up the narrows

        (who after all knows
                where the poem is and how

       ~

it comes towards you—): you climb one foot
after another. Hauling

          shadow. Motes of resemblance that demand

        that the flower release itself: just there, within.
Without, gravely white.

       ~

Rain darkens the graveled stone. Twice in the night
lightning.

THE SHUT ROSE

1 The Shadow

Then the knockings, the lights in houses, the barn doors

I could not spell
I could not run
My heart murmured:

                                        all that is in the eye:

My feet are so small they make no tracks
In the sand

Pretty bird, pretty bird

2 Without any irritable reaching after fact and reason

Through the window I see you reading—
Lift the latch, ah gently, ah tenderly, my sweet

I dreamed I was born in a boat
Smooth wood: (who can imagine

At sea

That one can be housed

Perfectly?)—

This is a word I said and I am looking into it

3 Pray you, tread softly

The ice hook swings

In thin air

Opens its mouth

And bites

My father lowers it gently

As if it were full of coins, full of heat

Full of broken line, frets

And promptings:

Who asked me for words I had not yet seen

4 A spell cannot be tattered & mended like a coat

Look, Mother. Look, Father.

All that remains now is—

Fathom,

                traversed by a simple girl—

I watch from the shade porch

(Radiance can make you weary,

Closing & opening, opening

& closing)

5 The shut rose shall dream of our loves and awake/
*   Full blown*

I am walking still

Walking further
                (and further)

Whom not having seen, I love:

Who withdraws from us

6 Felt the meadows the light held inside its flowing

A boat bangs the rocks, empty.
No rider. No paddle.

(How softly summer shuts with the creaking of a door)

Little clocks beating

*7 If the transitive be but the minor, we shall need a large
accession of strength, for the major sweetness*

I stir
soup in the red pot. Then I need only the spare
room, the one at the top of the house.

Booty of the dove.

PASQUEFLOWERWINDFLOWERPRAIRIESMOKEFLOWER
Anemone patens Anemone nemorosa Geum triflorum

As if well-spring
of glory

Each thing is merely the limit of the flame
To which it owes existence

And she,
who?

~

Leaving its mark
On the substance of the body settling

Inside the stem and elongation
Of soul:

Pain is also composed of the memory of good,
Its smoke shuttling

And feathery

~

The uses of resurrection speak shadow enough
(Speaks true who speaks shadow)

~

Wild-blooming, wind-flower
Stretched between worlds, silken,

Willed to make: your ripeness

Weighs lightly

SOLOMON'S SEAL
Polygonatum biflorum

And forth the particulars of rapture come—

words for want: underbrush twig drought
      withered wild rose:
            a sudden up-gathering of lance-like green
                  the flower turning

within shadow toward shadow away
      into shadow as if to say: here,
           here *was* my beauty. Then, *as if*—
                a fastening—

[When a person's mind is touched by me, I am her beginning]:

Trust the axis
Of my stem, summoning
Yourself through line to the drawing
Of matter, your
Keening to be—
      Let out into—

           [Let out: then, ask after—
              as if asking after

Would make
      the particular

          Into harmony—]:

*[When I begin to touch her mind, she may say to herself, 'What is
        happening to me?'*
                        Then I touch again.]

The flash of it as a flash of fire like a seal upon your heart like a seal
upon your arm the flash of it as a flash of fire a flame beauty a flame
like a seal upon your heart of Yahweh

                                        the flash of it like a seal upon
your arm for love is strong as death the flash of it as a flash of fire
like a seal—

                        Its roots can leave your mouth tingling and numb.
When the stalk is broken, a scar forms.

                                        [When she feels my touch,
she hastens to me.]
                        [God Salt.]

[Like the hart to the water-brook.]

                                        Gently constrained
In such a way that the light could not reach the darkness nor
darkness the light:

Eclipsing—

BLOODROOT
Sanguinaria canadensis

I am taking my time in wild wood

I forgot that I had bodily eyes
My petals drop for lack of nectar I am not seasonal

Nor manifold nor bounded
Here, here the heart—

Green leaves wrap around the flower stalk

I could give a contrary reading

The pod-like capsules split heavy with brown seed

To think is to cause something to appear to oneself
A folding like sound within the ear

Opening-after-bloom—
                              Where-from, where-to

To be so wrapped so held in body
Bent-in-space—

A formal freedom could appear

Perennial, of native
Composition

Do not lift me from the wild

Thing-fast and

Bleeding—

HER YOUNG DEATH / LOOSE / IN YOU

For the living wind that is the soul enters into this form, the body,

Strengthens it, makes it capable

Of life and wanders around within it like a caterpillar

That spins silk—

~

From which it is covered and closed in

As with a house.

In this form, the spirit

Of life discerns where the soul can divide,

Bend, turn about and fall into completeness. In just time,

The soul yearns for that of which it is shadow.

Who sees the inner things.

Ardently.

~

Death is a straitening. Even your skin weeps.

We lift out bone by elegant bone. I wish to be

Heartless and specific.

Wind blows our eyelashes dry.

In shifting snow, we find a weird intensive care.

All that is left after hard reckoning: our mouths

Punk with silence. In that new

Burning, pure

Calcium phosphate, whitely sterile.

We stand in the midst of the measuring

Table, smuggling order.

~

Mutability is within the soul itself. It listens its way in

With eager mouth. God was never so economical.

Death inscribes its signature without blot.

It's no fool.

I know now there is earth

Inside us. Ash.

Shame is when you turn

Your head away from something you do not want,

But did. Ash. In your hands.

Ash.

In the eye no washing will remove.

Necessity is

Our only testy mother.

BEFORE THE SPRING IN WHICH THE FORSYTHIA BLOOM AND SHE UNRAVELS ALL HER CHAMBERS, MOTHER WRITES

I will not let my knees bow nor my hands be lifted up
she said I am

Asleep or absent in the snowy hills
following rules for order as if they were new wool

In hand in whose comparison all whites are ink
and nothing

In motion shall clarify: at your first waking, *straight frame*
Thyself, she said, and careful:

We're born naked, all the rest is drag

I put away the silk virtue being made out of shadow
not cloth and note

The peculiar
accuracy of its knife and sharps—

It puts the heart in my chest on bloody wings—

And pull up the tent pegs like the Russian olive
in its shaky winter idiom

I keep moving, employed as scrivener: what you do
And say when you are lost

Is how you are found

DARK IS THE SHADOW OF ME

She knew him then and said to him, "Rabbuni!"
And Jesus said to her, "Do not cling to me."

(JOHN 20.17)

DARK IS THE SHADOW OF ME

1

She says, do not
Cling to me. And he says,
Do.

She and *he*
Differ. And yet,
Not so.

Sudden lexical
Gaps and looseness.
Habits of detour

Such that
I want to shuffle
My brain,

Put my hand
Down inside, spell
Some kind of
Awake.

A mistake is
A form of
Pilgrimage or a suffering
In place
Of elegy.

The soul is a verb. Not a noun.

2

Dark is the shadow of me.
Necessary and

Quick
Like the white curtain suddenly drawn

In the small house in deep summer when all is lake-light
Except the shadow

Of the arm that bends to embrace what we do
Not know we know.

3

Dark is a simple

Room. Within,
Concentric burning hearts. Back-lit city

Of scarlet solitudes where keening breathes
Open and out

Like a lung. Or rather—,
An eye containing an eye, the thing kissed

Into, hand in the small
Of the back

In-folding grace—

4

Common with nothing, nothing

At all, though fastened
Like the poppy,

To its feathery bursting forth.

Heart-house
Broken all over me.

5

Once I was afraid of the dark.

I needed marginalia to clarify.

I wanted signs along the highway and reversible simile.

If grief is a place and absence a place, and solitude
With its many burning walls—

                        I could not finish the sentence.

I wanted to burn.

What is the wind, what is it? How many windows?

I fill the dark with eyes.

6

She says, do not cling to me.
He says, do.

I remember how
Resurrection works.

Its marrow.
Its dark.
Its other-wise. Slow

Motion in plenitude.
No mourning
Cup.

7

Time falls over
Each frail
Symmetry

The hidden

Brick
Cracked sills and
Meticulous cut

Of God Salt

Summons
Form unto itself: the face upon the table or the shackled
Fence

For observation and
Quiet

Admonition: don't be
Selved-up—

Only that which in itself is place can accord place.

8

Also form may accord
The body

Its reconstruction—:

I don't know what dust is

Let alone
The dark

I have no mastery here
Just soot

And smother

I cannot breathe—

Meaning is such hard country.

9

The dove rebuilds
Her nest in shadow her low sound

Audible tenderness

And so I say to you

Words you can keep:
If it be
Now—

If it be not,
Now—

Suites and variations

To break to break to break the murmuring heart.

10

Who accords such place?
Who brings closure?

Who can imagine the pediment of shadow?
Its hush?

Its compressive strength?
The dust that can cast you across the street?

11

Jeremiah knew a God
As close as this is dangerous.

Fine pearl.
Likely to catch. And limn, then fade

The appearance of scars.

12

Black is not achieved in harsh light.
It is a shadow

Within shadow.

13

Just as the lake does not have tide in the same way as the sea,
So dark has its secret contour

And motion, its fog and perinatal
Remains

I press through it
Without seams

Without arms simple wind-wash
Of brain

Gathering syntax

And fear and seed-loosening beauty

The soul is a verb
Not a noun

But in whose grammar?

14

Do I need amulets here?
Or a stranger manual? Ancient guides to travel? Or whole colonies
Of oyster-catchers who eat at dusk

For offering?

15

The red-winged blackbird,
Tufted and

Private, bends the brown
Reeds at lake edge.

Does she gather votive to herself
As she lifts her
Tiny bones?

Or like the bee, tuck her head
Into the dark

Center, willful and
Surrendered

To the practice of awe?

The soul is a verb.
Not a noun.

16

Dark is the shadow of me, he says. Do not
Cling to me.

She says,
Do. Tenderness is never
Barren.

Like the gazelle
On the mountains of the covenant.

Like the needle in a compass.
Swung to.

17

Dark, like a fossil, leaves
Traces

Of signature, *terra amata*,
In mutant

And scorched possession.
Cling

To me.
Do.

Slowly, slowly, without
Rummage,

Without hanging on,
Without—

Luminous, without
Body,

Ever.
Not a wing fluttering.

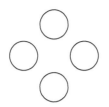

SHADOW OF TWO

1

Among the forms, no form. Only the leisure

Of regret, a kind of dry

2

Reckoning, not unlike the sky in late October when the turning

Comes. I ask, what is the form

3

Of desire? She says he forgot to make spring within

The wreckage. I know the hard

4

Fact that forgiveness contains no erasure, only forfeit.

It bites. I huddle against its surface and grind

5

And stir, my fury, a scrupulous ghost.

6

Is desire, then, I ask, a heaven where there is only shadow

Of two? The sign

7

That something has been present, a filling in

Between the lines

8

Of self and apposite stillness? Is it that kind of knowing

That is like the painting

9

Of the eyes of the Buddha—: you must climb

The ladder, turn away

10

And paint his eyes while looking in a mirror.

What you see

11

Is then removed enough to survive

Your error. Then you may climb down the ladder and

12

Admit your want.

THERE IS WORK TO DO
WITHIN NOTHINGNESS

There is a creature, among all others, one
within whose voice there is a secret voice
which once heard
unlocks the door that unlocks the mountain.

—FRANK BIDART

Nox nihil donat.
Nothing is night's gift.

—ANNE CARSON

THE DAY IS BREAKING SOMEONE ELSE'S HEART

We speak of signs as if tending them would yield
up simples—

watch the lake pitch down and open its body wide,
then close and sink upwards into a low

slip of moon, combing its deep-tide, its peels
and shingle.

Someone said water has margins. They slide
like monotonies. Or hungers.

Deceive the eye. As in a photograph.
Or rue.

On TV, a city burns. The sky, blood orange. I turn the house
lights off one by one. The sap lines run.

The clock chimes the after hour on long spinner legs.
Lady sings the blues.

I talk now only of small things.
A dragonfly stutters, yett-yett, yett-yett against the screen door.

I did not know this would happen—

Wild blue aster to my waist.

AND SO, HOW DOES ONE LEARN HOW TO DROWN?

Like the blossom of the cherry tree unfolding from its good

offices light falls out of spring green within the lung an unclasping
which runs under water: one hears singing in the silt.

Humble lectors in a labor of notice: the skin goes
brown and blush and earthly—

and wishes *oh be* and
let not: not—, *yet:* no hindering.

I cannot choose my treasure: *Thou shalt—and thou*
Shalt—
In the long grass and scrub I am shoring

My portion and loose papers. Settling raw. Shambling into sunken
traceries. And splint.

OF SOUL I KEEP MARGINS

utterly free, feet shod
for grievous walking: all

erasable footing, loose sheets of water, white
letters (your mark) in a black field.

I make preparation for the wake of breathing,
costly, perfect spillage & stumbling.

What if beauty is only a settling, a practiced
disruption polished to dangerous gloss?

I set my foot down to keep the index of bruising
tender to its supple edge. Trace

a wing.
Listen for the long hollow cry of the goose.

THERE BE PHANTASIES

The hermit thrush whistles in the morning

[no harm] [no harm]

as there be phantasies
in wavering wemens wit

that none can tell,

I file endurance and wing-work

            under fiction

the little churchyard with its lamenting names

            under hunger

[Thou must now know further]

[?] made three seasons, summer
and winter and autumn third
and fourth spring when
there is blooming but to eat enough
is not

[no harm] [no harm]

[Or we run ourselves] [aground]

I file chafing of wax (Oh seal upon my heart)

                    under inquisition, bootless

Magic garment

                    under provision

Comfort, under

                    barren ground, long heath, broom,
                    furze, anything

[Thou must now know] [further]

To eat enough
is not

                    under hand
                    under water

Oh, the Cry

[did knock against my heart]
[did knock against my heart]

                    under blooming

TERRA AMATA

I, a blind daughter, whisper to the dark
Are you my home? Are you my mother?

—Ye Chun

Who, just who, is blind
In the story where the girl becomes a tree?

> *She can run she can run into the green forest and change*
> *Herself change how she is her skin*
> *   her eyes hands ears like a genetic*

> *Pilgrim of cells traveling, but not homeward—*

~

Who is it who said darkness is a form of metonymy?

~

If that is the case, then her beauty, that girl, her change, is
a form of vault,

Like the arc of an eagle on the hunt,
through which she investigates the lines and ash

Of herself, the kind of hunger (what eye sees,
the hand wants):

That makes a quilt out of scrap
and sews from the torn pieces, (stitching two over two under

Then pull tight) guilt and
passio:

(I suffer, she says, oh) (And oh, I can sail
straight into nothing):

> *(If the word comes slowly, wait,*
> *for come it will, without*
> *fail—).*

It is a kind of fasting to become another thing:
you, vermiculate,

Spine
subtracted to birch

And coddled.
(Or was it the red ash to which she was burned?)

So that she hurt twice, the first within
her change.

The second, in the act of knowing
that her new self would blot the generosity of her strange

beauty.
Like a watermark, that first self, carefully pressed within.

As if birch bark curled by wind, her body resists
sudden eclipse.

Then adheres to the knife.
Still, now,

She carries her ruin.

I SWIM A SEA THAT HAS NO SHORE OR BOTTOM

Or pouring-out:—or blown egg-white—brown

Birds picking seed from my heart—

> *[Take a little peece of a Spunge, or a Linnen*
> *being cleane without any soyle:. . . , and it will out,*
> *and within—]*

Blue cone flower and dirt that tastes like salt

~

Whatever was:

[Nombre de agua]

~

My soul, slat-backed like a prim chair
[It is blank here, for Reasons]: after the plow

Breaking, the rain.

AND SOMEONE SAID ABOUT ECSTASY:
IT IS A LONELINESS

To reckon with—
As if she could clothe herself by falling

Down a well.
Blood-bloom is not a property of awe

Or fit of frail sense. Like elegy,
She whispers evenly *nothing comes from nothing,*

Speak
Against abbreviation.

The room gathers to *between*—

~

How, then, this *after-place,*
Half-lit:

If scar tissue, *if* the clock still ticks at the hour, or the bees,
Swarm in apple blossom,

Then their settling, all *if: if* yield to, *if* toward

Honey-comb, *if* make murmur—

The hive is for where the honey was—:

Sloot-plain of orange,
                              light-wildering.

GIRL AT THE GREAT LAKE

So that everyday it fills   draft, lave & frenetic
room that is itself

~

This girl all accident all
instead of

~

Full of little mirrors   sheer weight
A beggary of air

~

This girl all accident all

~

Asks, which earth am I in?

The clock strikes three
Hand-in-the-light

~

Instead of

The little sentences I began & never finished—
the little wells I dug & never filled—

~

Two sheets of paper laid, cream with blue rule
in ink and pencil, a salutation, formal
& hushed

having put myself by like a jar of pears
in thin air

~

The shelf is crowded now
Tomatoes hurry their color
They await the picking

~

This girl all accident all
instead of

~

Out there, the underface   burns
leaves no silt

In drift and out of hand

PILEATED

Flying lightly
        they hurry
                over the broken

Skin of poplar, white
        underwing, wingbeats
                flashing—what if—

What if each—
        thing of the natural
                world were a talking stone—

I am training the stems to my flowers

I am working, lingering even so that you stay near

What if the hurried call—
        kik-kikkik-kik-kik—
                what if it could tell—

What if it could say with exactitude,
        even sympathy,
                calling out in the old way—

Pity moving together with pity,
its diggings, its oblong holes

Three red and crested heads
                figure of beaked
                        mortality & blur

Dread energy unspooling, weightless
Like a solitude, multiplying

Spare fact in the mottled rumble of privacy

The dyings have been too deep for me

I was afraid, said Adam, and hid himself from beauty

The tree split for burning

As if there were no fire

As if there were only

This

GOODNESS, SWEET, CAN MAKE YOU BLIND

As does that radiance in the whelming, common
measure of presence

rendered & washed
to which my body summons me.

In the letting out, the sense of soul faulted
by sudden sentence,

we will not know you, that left me
Night-crawler.

Even Pity laughed—

Need is the form of your unraveling, she said, plain
speech with lost rules of usage.

The wells have fallen in and have inhabitants—

Who's to decide where the period goes.
Or if such raw marks serve.

RUDE PRAYER

You say: Admit the presence of tears—

I say: Gesture affords entrance. It makes.

You say: The stars are flying apart. Cold at the core, the body.

I say: There are new tattoos. It hums around here.

You say: ENTER WOUND.

I say: I'll break. And flap my hands. Their bloody knuckles.
The furniture is in the fireplace!

You say: FINE. I'm dancing like God. I haven't eaten in a long
time. Move the furniture.

I say: I'm cold. Oh for God's sake! Where's the room of halt?
I need to load the canoe.

You say: I don't know where the dying begins. This is not
the worst.

I say: Hurry up. Where was I when we passed each other?

You say: Wound is the tough mark of grace. Invite dark night
for supper. Pilfer.

I say: At the next moon, put leaves in your mouth.

You say: Sleep on a stone.

I say: There are new tattoos. Slow soul that I am—
I want reply.

THE LETTER *I*, THAT IS, SMALL AND LARGE

1

The playwright says

He was trying to write a play that would get him killed.
Good Irish boy. Wants to be on top of the list

For death and dismemberment. True test of art.

No hands.

2

It's March. The little girl in the blue dress comes in out of the rain.
She says it's pouring down God in here. She uses

Capitals to establish boundaries.

3

I want an egg, she says. The letter I is small and large.
I am sight reading.

No hands.

4

She eats her egg spilling yellow
All over herself.

5

The mother, her arms full of day old bread, says if
My child learns what is sweet,

She will want it.

THE MOON GROWS RED IN ITS REEDS

The blackbirds, red-winged & proprietary, observe
carefully what is set before them

They eat with greed, make mean fences
Know they must provide—

They do not give way

~

Keeping of things, they say, is to make
deliverance: plaint of dust and *turab*, bullet

And skin, cinnamon and ginger. Breach.

Bone attracts some creatures

~

Everything dies in the same way
Star and apple tree
                    And after midnight

No hand no limb no face no whinnying

No cipher

EVERMORE THE NIGHT BIRD CALLS OUT
IN THE BARE BRANCHES

Its sound so long and pure I turn towards the evening
light which like the chameleon

Alters its color so it can steal the heart and dim.
The cows lie under the black oak expecting only rain,

Having that property
in themselves that does not change, but is a kind

Of dull stability. Of a sudden they rise
and move upwards, lifting

Their bulk, following the dark line of the hill toward the slender
ghost of new moon. *As I say: this world.*

The barn stays for them next the shallows,
fitful and green.

THE DESERT HAS TWELVE THINGS

You shall nothingness love.

                                 You shall somethingness flee.

Yet hold thingness in hand.

~

Emptied of wind-singing, spectral—

~

Made of bruised bones: stand alone, go to no one,
drink—

~

Winds grow from many directions. Pay attention.
Error can be fatal here.

~

The instruction of wandering sands: forgetting has its uses. Sand carries
everyone off equally. Like death.

~

Crown – of – Thorns *(Euphorbia milii):* inflorescence is composed
of a specialized structure.

Crosses are collected in the wild.

~

Stars press between worlds the nothing that is not there
And the nothing that is.

~

Emptiness does not disperse here, does not scatter.
It collects finely.

~

It is here it is there it is far it is near it is deep it is high.
It exists in such a way that is neither this nor that.

~

Desert has no proof-text.
It corrects itself in division and motion of light and sand.

Just so, soul repeats and corrects in the way it divides and
Turns and sifts within.

~

Stars make material the presence of cleaving.

WORKING METHODS

1

You say you want to know what beauty is: that its shadow broke
in the afternoon sun,

that you came so close you almost set yourself on fire and could not
be put out,

that you saw in that burning, that flickering light, the disparity
between the perfect and the imperfect.

Then you wept.
You knew, in that instant, *breakage,*

whatever its cause, is the dark complement
to the act of making:

one implies the other. Like soapstone: metamorphic
and without melt.

2

Jacob could not explain what he saw when he wrestled with the angel.
Damage left its hollow

mark of grace. What he did not know, could not see, is that the struggle
to hold the numinous

is to stand on the margins between what is mortal
and what is not.

Nothing left for him after, but the breathing of the touched—
Breathing out, breathing in.

And then to prize the insufficiency
of his too courteous dream.

Pain is an appetite
for comforting of just this kind. As if scalded

by that strange privacy, he must have stood, called
out some newly taught

word, brushed off the angel ash, the godly broth—
soul, half-turned to rupture—

3

Just as the painter carefully thins the ground of her canvas
and arrives

at the place where her hand can make its surface speak
and husk the grammar of her fluency,

just as the surgeon touches the outer skin of the heart, then plunges
the knife into the valve

to explore its remains, so too, you repair the reach of your soul.
Your hand proposes,

depends upon the semblance of
the invisible.

DEATH MIGHT DEPRIVE ME OF TIME

A wound is necessary.

~

Nevertheless, I would give you a pattern for a perfect day.
Argument, a field of blue bells. Thickly finite.

~

When I am not and you are, recall the hunger of me.
Believe it.

I am open like the fraying of twilight, foraging and wakeful—
My sentence: to be eaten

word by word. And this, this eating, licit
as late rain.

~

Let your heart
be kept always in awe of this

by continual remembering that you have no form
of prayer [for desire].

~

I brush the green blade of your skin with milk lifting from my salt sleep.

~

It is a wash of gold. That was.

~

Pick your way through radiance with dirty shoes.

THERE IS WORK TO DO WITHIN NOTHINGNESS

A simple solitude: slow light seams the land.
The great bird turns upon the thermal.

Its aloneness, unrestrained, fiercely elegant.
It knows no shallow places.

It cannot hold back.
Even its smallest feathers hook the air.

~

The lake keeps watch for the legible
footprint of matter.

I worry to move over it and slip
my paddle in, let the water fold back upon itself.

The curve of falling water demands something of us
we had not perceived. We write by hand.

~

My hand mars the heart-gray surface. It scatters
the admissible.

Someone said *Ruin is formal.*
White linen, necessary. Also, the collapse of beauty.

~

Its white head turning, its yellow eyes prepared for reading
rooms made of water upright and edged.

Where we land, loosestrife and pale
anemone.

All three of us locked deep in shadow and silt.

Which is the abler soul?

~

Telling, telling parts of the heart, the lake breathes,
hurries us, its foot on the treadle.

My hand cannot hold what it contains. We move
in tidal wind.

The lake comes to fetch me to underwater work.
Granite stones catch fire.

I trace pools of light, watch a brown spider navigate
the lake-skin. It walks as if on nothing.

Each step, intimate and careful
and sheer.

~

Voyager travels between the stars. Up there to know
what is between is to know—

Yet, we are far, far outside.
Vacant. Inscribed.

Ground-figures singing like they do in opera:
Give me, give me back the night.

~

The great bird comes to rest in white pine.
The sun sinks down through upturned branches.

Fretting the light.

~

Shadowfall.
Where my hand was no longer is: *anima mundi*.

I leave no trace.

A MAP TO AFTER

Silence keeps its winter axis.

I want to make a map. For arrival in a wind so fierce
It looks as if the moon is burning, its stem trailing dark matter.

They say, *where* is an invention, a composition
Of latitude and longitude.
Even detour.

I want a coastal route from you to you,
Inlets and tidal marsh, where salt hay grows and folds up
In thick rolling mats of green.

I will pick sea lavender, ox-eye and aster to mark
The rearrangement of ourselves, all that climbing to the flats,
And circulation through and out again.

We will hear our breathing. Watch a moon snail
Suck the life out of clam. And the ribbed
Mussels cling to marsh grass. Signage that sings

In low voice: if I were pitch pine—
If I were prickly pear, if I were glossy buckthorn—
If I were cord grass, if I were ox-eye, if I were

Night blooming morning glory, *ipomoea alba*—
If I were slow moving, freshly tidal, and still she—

Whose inflorescence is branched.

NOTES

OF GOD SALT

God Salt is a metaphor used by Cormac McCarthy in *The Road*: "He walked out into the road. The silence. The *salitter* drying from the earth" (p. 220). *Salitter* was first used by Jakob Boehme, a 16th c. German theologian: "This . . . drying, I call . . . the divine SALITTER . . . the seed of the whole Deity, and . . . as it were a mother, which receiveth the seed, and always generateth fruit again, according to the qualities of the seed" (*Aurora*, 11.87); "And this, in the deep of the Father, is like a divine SALITTER . . . which I must needs liken to the earth, which before its corruption was even such a *salitter*" (*Aurora*, 4.8).

PRAIRIE, UNDER FULL MOON: "O sparrow" is from Dan Beachy-Quick's *This Nest, Swift Passerine*, p. 33.

MANTRA: The refrain is from Anne Carson's *Nox*. The waggle dance of the bee is mentioned by David Seymour in his poem "Impressions" in *Lyric Ecology*, p. 255.

ANALOGY OF THE BEE AND THE SOUL: Lines 9-11 are from an unpublished poem by Rilke, cited in Martin Heidegger's *Poetry, Language and Thought*, p. 99. Lines 15-16 reference Rilke's "Ninth Elegy" in *The Collected Poetry of Rainer Maria Rilke*, p. 199; lines 19-20 are a refract of several lines in Rilke's "Eighth Elegy," p. 193; line 21 is from Rilke's "I am, O Anxious One," p. 3. All translations are by Stephen Mitchell. The image of the wall not opened by the doorkeeper is from Hildegard of Bingen's *Scivias*, Book Three, Vision 6, p. 393. Translated by Columba Hart and Jane Bishop.

MERCY AS A FORM OF ECONOMY: The first couplet is from Paul Celan's *The Meridian*, p. 148. The stanza in italics is from Dan Beachy-Quick's *A Whaler's Dictionary*, p. 292.

COLUMBINE, WILD: The epigraph is from Hildegard of Bingen's "Hymn to the Holy Spirit" in *Symphonia*, p.143. Translated by Barbara Newman.

BLAZING STAR, WILD: Line 13 is an adaptation of a sentence in Hildegard of Bingen's *Scivias*, Book One, Vision 5, pp. 135-136.

SALT FLOWER: Stanza 6 is from "North" by Carl Phillips in *The Rest of Love*, p. 38. Stanza 9 is a variation of Rilke's line "And never Nowhere without the No" in "The Eighth Elegy," *The Collected Poetry of Rainer Maria Rilke*, p. 138. Translated by Stephen Mitchell.

TRILLIUM: Line 6 is from David Seymour's "Impressions" in *Lyric Ecology*, p. 254. Lines in italics in stanza 3 are adapted from Mechthild of Magdeburg's "The Desert Has Twelve Things" in *The Flowing Light of the Godhead*, Book I, p. 55. Translated by Frank J. Tobin.

THE SHUT ROSE: The titles in sections 2-6 are borrowed from John Keats' letter on negative capability, written to his brothers; Emily Dickinson's letter 663; John Keats' song "Hush, hush, tread softly!"; Jorie Graham's "Easter Morning Aubade" and Emily Dickinson's letters 665 and 654.

PASQUEFLOWERWINDFLOWER: The second couplet quotes Rodin. (See Bachelard.) "Speaks true who speaks shadow" is from Paul Celan's *Selected Poems and Prose*, p. 77. Translated by John Felstiner. "Your ripeness weighs lightly" is from "Sequence for St. Rupert" in Hildegard of Bingen's *Symphonia*, p. 195.

SOLOMON'S SEAL: Line 1 is from "Notes towards a Supreme Fiction," Wallace Stevens. Other lines in italics are adapted from Hildegard of Bingen's *Scivias*, Book Three, Vision 8, pp. 428-430. Translated by Columba Hart and Jane Bishop.

HER YOUNG DEATH / LOOSE / IN YOU: The title is from Anne Carson's "As tree shapes from mist" in *Men in the Off Hours*, p. 43. Stanza 1 and stanza 2 are refracts from Hildegard of Bingen's *Causae et Curae in Holistic Healing*, p. 56. Translated by Mary Palmquist.

BEFORE THE SPRING IN WHICH THE FORSYTHIA BLOOM: The sentence "We're born naked, all the rest is drag" is from RuPaul's *Lettin It All Hang Out: An Autobiography*. "It puts the heart in my chest on bloody wings" is from Sappho's Fragment 31. Translated by Anne Carson in *Decreation*, p. 159. Other phrases in italics are from Elizabeth Joscelin's *Legacy to Her Unborn Child*, 1622 (British Library, Additional Manuscript 27, 467).

DARK IS THE SHADOW OF ME

DARK IS THE SHADOW OF ME: In Part 1, "The soul is a verb . . ." is from David Mitchell's *The Thousand Autumns of Jacob de Zoet*, p. 146. In Part 5, "If grief is a place" is from Laurie Sheck's *A Monster's Notes*, p. 55. In Part 5, "What is the wind" is from Gertrude Stein's *Tender Buttons*. In Part 7, "Only that which in itself is place can accord place" is from Heidegger's "Building Dwelling Thinking" in *Poetry, Language and Thought* as translated by Gustaf Sobin in *Luminous Debris*, p. 198. Part 12 is adapted from Andy Goldsworthy's *Stone*, p. 64.

THERE IS WORK TO DO WITHIN NOTHINGNESS

THE DAY IS BREAKING SOMEONE ELSE'S HEART: The title is from James Merrill's "Prism" in *Collected Poems*, p.138.

THERE BE PHANTASIES: The translation of Alkman Fragment 20 is by Anne Carson in "Essay On What I Think About Most" in *Men in the Off Hours*, pp. 30-36.

TERRA AMATA: Excerpt from the poem "Sunflower" by Ye Chun, from *Travel Over Water* (The Bitter Oleander Press, 2005), is printed by permission of the author. "Darkness is a form of metonymy" is adapted from G. C. Waldrep's "Apologia Pro Vita Tua" in *New American Writing*, Issue 27.

I SWIM A SEA THAT HAS NO SHORE OR BOTTOM: The title is from Petrarch 212. The first quotation is from Robert Triplet's *Writing Tables with a Kalender* in "Hamlet's Tables and the Technologies of Writing" by Peter Stallybrass et. al. in *SQ*, 55.4.

AND SOMEONE SAID ABOUT ECSTASY: The title is from Jack Gilbert's "Naked Except for the Jewelry" in *Refusing Heaven*, p. 4. Line 16 is from Carl Phillips' "The Rest of Love" in *The Rest of Love*, p. 11.

GIRL AT THE GREAT LAKE: "This girl all accident all instead of" is from Jorie Graham's "Pollock and Canvas" in *The End of Beauty*, p. 83.

GOODNESS, SWEET, CAN MAKE YOU BLIND: "The wells have fallen in and have inhabitants" is from W. S. Merwin's "Some Last Questions" in *Second Four Books of Poems*, p. 83.

THE LETTER *I*, THAT IS, SMALL AND LARGE: The title is from John Banville's *The Sea*, p. 52.

THE MOON GROWS RED IN ITS REEDS: Line in italics in stanza 2 is from Michael Ondaatje's *Anil's Ghost*, p. 73. Lines in italics in stanza 3 are from Nelly Sachs' "Music in the ears of the dying" in *The Seeker*, p. 143.

EVERMORE THE NIGHT BIRD CALLS OUT IN THE BARE BRANCHES: The title is from John Banville's *The Sea*, p. 48.

THE DESERT HAS TWELVE THINGS: The title and stanza 1 are from Mechthild of Magdeburg's *The Flowing Light of the Godhead*, p. 55. "It is here it is there it is far it is near . . ." is from Meister Eckhart's "Granum Sinapis." Translated by Bernard McGinn in *The Essential Writings of Christian Mysticism*, p. 294.

WORKING METHODS: "Breakage, whatever its cause . . ." is from Louise Glück's *Proofs & Theories: Essays on Poetry*, 75. ". . . as if pain were an appetite for comforting of just this kind" is from Marilynne Robinson's *Home*, p. 64.

DEATH MIGHT DEPRIVE ME OF TIME: The title and lines in italics are adapted from Elizabeth Joscelin's *Legacy to Her Unborn Child*, 1622 (British Library, Additional Manuscript 27, 467).

THERE IS WORK TO DO WITHIN NOTHINGNESS: The title is from Dan Beachy-Quick's *A Whaler's Dictionary*, p. 179.

A MAP TO AFTER: The title is from Dan Beachy-Quick's *Spell*, p. 36.

EPIGRAPHS

"Markings" in Seamus Heaney's *Seeing Things*. London: Faber and Faber, 1991, p. 9.

Excerpt from "Sanjaya at 17" from *Watching the Spring Festival* by Frank Bidart. Copyright © 2008 Frank Bidart. Reprinted by permission of Farrar, Straus and Giroux, LLC.

Two lines from Anne Carson's *Nox*, *Nox nihil donat. / Nothing is night's gift.*, reprinted by permission of New Directions Publishing.

BIBLIOGRAPHY

Bachelard, Gaston. *Psychoanalyis of Fire*. Trans. Alan C. M. Ross. Boston: Beacon Press, 1964.

Beachy-Quick, Dan. *A Whaler's Dictionary*. Minneapolis: Milkweed Editions, 2008.

---. *Spell*. Boise, Idaho: Ahsahta Press, 2004.

---. *This Nest, Swift Passerine*. North Adams, MA: Tupelo Press, 2009.

Banville, John. *The Sea*. New York: Knopf, 2005.

Boehme, Jakob. *Aurora or Day-Spring*. Trans. John Sparrow. London: Printed by John Streater, for Giles Calvert. 1656. Ed. C.J. Borker and D.S. Hehner. Electronic Text Edition, 2009. Ed. Martin Euser. PDF. 24 Nov. 2014 <http://Meuser. awardspace.com.html>.

Carson, Anne. *Decreation*. New York: Knopf, 2005.

---. *Men in the Off Hours*. New York: Knopf, 2000.

---. *Nox*. New York: New Directions Publishing, 2010.

Celan, Paul. *Selected Poems and Prose*. Trans. John Felstiner. New York: W. W. Norton, 2001.

---. *The Meridian*. Ed. Bernhard Boschenstein and Heino Schmull. Trans. Pierre Joris. Stanford: Stanford University Press, 2011.

Chun, Ye. *Travel Over Water*. Fayetteville, NY: The Bitter Oleander Press, 2005.

Eckhart, Meister. "Granum Sinapis" in *Essential Writings of Christian Mysticism*. New York: Random House, 2006.

Gilbert, Jack. *Refusing Heaven*. New York: Knopf, 2005.

Glück, Louise. *Proofs and Theories*. New York: Ecco Press, 1995.

Goldsworthy, Andy. *Stone*. New York: Abrams, 1994.

Graham, Jorie. *The End of Beauty*. New York: The Echo Press, 1987.

Heidegger, Martin. *Poetry, Language and Thought*. New York: Harper & Row, 1971.

Hildegard of Bingen. *Causae et Curae*. Trans. Priscilla Throop. MedievalMS. 2012.

---. *Scivias*. Trans. Columba Hart and Jane Bishop. New York: Paulist Press, 1990.

---. *Symphonia*. Trans. Barbara Newman. Ithaca, NY: Cornell University Press, 1988.

Joscelin, Elizabeth. *Legacy to Her Unborn Child*. British Library, Additional Manuscript 27, 467.

McCarthy, Cormac. *The Road*. New York: Vintage International, 2006.

McGinn, Bernard, ed. *Essential Writings of Christian Mysticism*. New York: Random House, 2006.

Mechthild of Magdeburg. *The Flowing Light of the Godhead, Book I.* Trans. Frank Tobin. New York: Paulist Press, 1998.

Merrill, James. *Collected Poems.* New York: Knopf, 2001.

Merwin, W.S. *Second Four Books of Poems.* Port Townsend, Washington: Copper Canyon Press, 1993.

Mitchell, David. *The Thousand Autumns of Jacob de Zoet.* New York: Random House, 2010.

Ondaatje, Michael. *Anil's Ghost.* New York: Vintage, 2001.

Palmquist, Mary. *Holistic Healing.* Collegeville: Liturgical Press, 1994.

Petrarch. *Sonnets and Shorter Poems.* Trans. David R. Slavitt. Cambridge: Harvard University Press, 2012.

Phillips, Carl. *The Rest of Love.* New York: Farrar, Straus and Giroux, 2004.

Rilke, Rainer Maria. *Collected Poems.* Trans. Stephen Mitchell. New York: Vintage Books, 1989.

Robinson, Marilynne. *Home.* New York: Picador Reprint, 2009.

RuPaul. *Lettin It All Hang Out: An Autobiography.* New York: Hyperion, 1996.

Sachs, Nelly. *The Seeker and Other Poems.* New York: Farrar, Straus and Giroux, 1970.

Seymour, David. "Impressions" in *Lyric Ecology*. Ed. Mark Dickinson and Clare Goulet. Toronto: Cormorant Books, 2010.

Sheck, Laurie. *A Monster's Notes*. New York: Knopf, 2009.

Sobin, Gustaf. *Collected Poems*. Greenfield, MA: Tasliman House, 2010.

---. *Luminous Debris*. Berkeley, CA: University of California Press, 1999.

Stallybrass, Peter, et. al. "Hamlet's Tables and the Technologies of Writing." *Shakespeare Quarterly* 55.4 (2004): 379-419.

Stein, Gertrude. *Tender Buttons*. Mineola, NY: Dover Publications, 1997. First published by Claire Marie. New York, 1914. www.bartleby.com/140/. 24 Nov. 2014.

Stevens, Wallace. *Notes Towards a Supreme Fiction*. Cummington, MA: Cummington Press, 1942.

Waldrep, G. C. "Apologia Pro Vita Tua." *New American Writing* 27 (2008).

ACKNOWLEDGMENTS

Many thanks to the editors of the journals in which versions of these poems appear:

Agni: "Shadow of Two," "The Letter *I*, that is, Small and Large." *Barrow Street*: "Rude Prayer." *Blue Mesa*: "Evermore the night bird calls out in the bare branches." *Cerise Press*: "The Shut Rose." *Crab Creek Review*: "Terra Amata." *Grove Review*: "Death Might Deprive Me of Time." *Gulf Coast*: "Her young death." *Hot Metal Bridge*: "I Swim a Sea That Has No Shore or Bottom." *Harvard Review*: "Before the Spring in Which the Forsythia Bloom." This poem also appeared in *Best New Poets 2008*. *Memorious*: "And So, How Does One Learn How to Drown," "Salt Flower." *Massachusetts Review*: "There Be Phantasies." *New England Review*: "Working Methods." *Notre Dame Review*: "Analogy of the Bee and the Soul," "Mantra," "Solomon's Seal," "The Day Is Breaking Someone Else's Heart." *Orion*: "Prairie, Under Full Moon." *Salamander*: "A Map to After." *Salmagundi*: "Girl at the Great Lake." *Spiritus*: "Of Soul, I Keep Margins." *Spoon River*: "Mercy as a Form of Economy." *Terrain*: "There is Work to Do Within Nothingness." *Water-Stone*: "Goodness, Sweet, Can Make You Blind," "Pileated." *Witness*: "The Moon Grows Red in Its Reeds."

Pushcart Prize Nominations: "Evermore the night bird calls out in the bare branches," "Death Might Deprive Me of Time," "The Shut Rose."

"Analogy of the Bee and the Soul" was commissioned by the College of Saint Benedict, St. Joseph, Minnesota, and set to music by Janika Vandervelde. (Hothouse Press, 2013.)

My thanks to fellow poets and novelists who read the manuscript and wrote blurbs for it: Hadara Bar-Nadav, Frank Bidart, Mary Gordon, Patricia Kirkpatrick, John Matthias, and Mary Pinard.

My thanks to Bernard McGinn, Patricia McGinn, for sources mystical, and Penny Gill, for political commentary and her wilderness home.

Thanks, and ever thanks, to Andrea Watson for her care, patience, and guidance through the deep thickets and re-seeing of each precious poem and the ordering of them into a whole.

My deep gratitude to my Loretto community at home and abroad, who have supported my teaching and creative work.

ABOUT THE AUTHOR

Eva Hooker is Professor of English and Writer in Residence at Saint Mary's College, Notre Dame, Indiana. *Notes for Survival in the Wilderness*, a hand bound chapbook, (Chapiteau Press, Montpelier, Vermont) was published in 2011. Lake Superior and Madeline Island have left their profound water-mark on the poems that make up this sequence. Her earlier chapbook, *The Winter Keeper* (Chapiteau Press, 2000) was a finalist for the Minnesota Book Award in poetry in 2001. Prior to her appointment at Saint Mary's, she was Regents Professor of Poetry at Saint John's University in Collegeville, Minnesota.

ALSO BY 3: A TAOS PRESS

Collecting Life: Poets on Objects Known and Imagined
Madelyn Garner and Andrea Watson

Seven
Sheryl Luna

The Luminosity
Bonnie Rose Marcus

Trembling in the Bones: A Commemorative Edition
Eleanor Swanson

3 A.M.
Phyllis Hotch

Ears of Corn: Listen
Max Early

Elemental
Bill Brown

Rootwork
Veronica Golos

Farolito
Karen S. Córdova